THE
POCKET

Geordie English

Published in 2024
by Gemini Adult Books Ltd
Part of Gemini Books Group

Based in Woodbridge and London
Marine House, Tide Mill Way
Woodbridge, Suffolk IP12 1AP
United Kingdom

www.geminibooks.com

Text and Design © 2024 Gemini Books Group
Part of the Gemini Pocket series

Cover image: Alamy/Steve Cukrow.

ISBN 978-1-83616-001-4

Printed in China

10 9 8 7 6 5 4 3 2 1

THE
POCKET

Geordie
English

G:

Contents

Introduction

Geordie, spoken in Newcastle and on the banks of the River Tyne in the county of Northumberland in the north-east of England, is one of the most easily recognisable British dialects. At one time it was rare to hear Geordie elsewhere in the UK, but TV programmes such as *Byker Grove*, footballers such as Paul Gascoigne and Alan Shearer, and the presenters Ant and Dec have helped to make it more widely known. From 'Howay, man!' to 'Haddaway!', become fluent in Newcastle English.

Geordie, which has its own distinctive vocabulary, grammar and pronunciation, remains the best preserved British dialect, largely because of its geographical isolation –

there are parts of Scotland which are further south than Northumberland. Many present-day features of Geordie were once present in other dialects, but these were mostly eradicated when the English language was standardised during the eighteenth century.

Further from the Tyne, the dialect becomes softer, sounding almost Cumbrian before the western boundary is reached; and in the colliery villages, a distinctive variety of Geordie, 'Pitmatic', is spoken, in which terms used in mining have entered everyday speech.

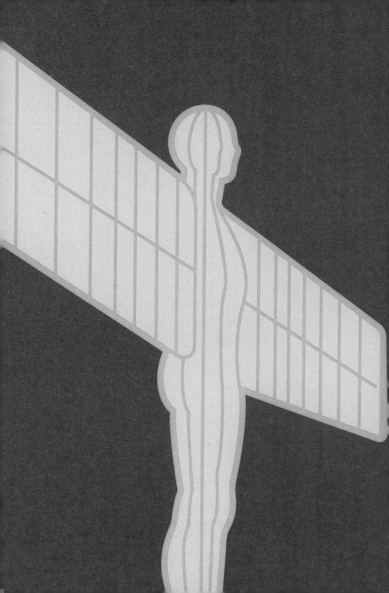

GEORDIE

-

ENGLISH

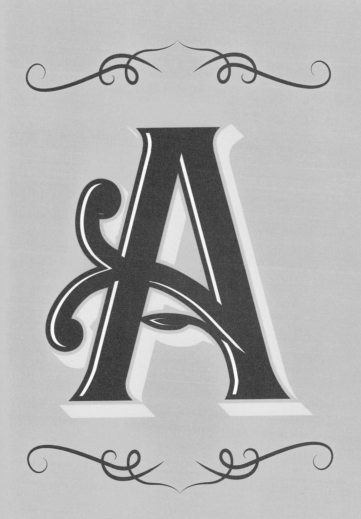

GEORDIE	ENGLISH
aadfashint	old-fashioned
aah	I, e.g., *aah will*
aakwad	awkward
aal	(i) all
	(ii) I will
aan	own, e.g., *mi aan hoose*
aback	behind, e.g., *he's aback the hoose*
abbut	yes but, e.g., *abbut aal not let ye*
afeard	afraid
ahaad	hold, e.g., *aal get ahaad ov it*
alang	along

GEORDIE	ENGLISH
amany	several
an aal	also
aneath	underneath
aside of	next to
at	(i) that, e.g., *them at's gan*
	(ii) for, e.g., *what ye stannin there at?*
	(iii) in, e.g., *aam at the hoose*
atween	between
aye	yes

GEORDIE	ENGLISH
babby	infant
backeend	autumn
back-gannin	getting worse
back-ower	return, e.g., *he came back-ower tiv us*
bad	sick (sometimes 'badly')
badly off	poor
bairn	young child
bait	snack, dinner, packed lunch
battered	tired
beastie	small animal
beck	stream
beggar	fellow, e.g., *whaas the little beggar noo?*
belta	really good
berrer-end	majority

GEORDIE	ENGLISH
bested	beaten
bi	by (when in front of a consonant, e.g., *his bi hissel*)
bide	endure, stand, e.g., *aah canna bide yon chap*
bin	been, e.g., *hoo ye bin the day?*
binno	by this time
bit	(i) small, short
	(ii) a short time

baal

football

Newcastle's team is known as the Magpies.

GEORDIE	ENGLISH
biv	by (when in front of a vowel, e.g., *better biv a mile*)
blate	shy, awkward
blythe	glad
bobby dazzler	something or someone excellent – you might also say, 'They're a real diamond.'
bonny	(i) good-looking
	(ii) pleasant disposition
	(iii) used to exaggerate the opposite of good, e.g., *thaas made a bonny mess*
	(iv) greeting, e.g., *hoo ye bin, bonny lad?*
booza	public house
bramma	perfect
brockle	frail, precarious, uncertain

GEORDIE	ENGLISH
by	next to, near to. Used together with other words, originally down the pit: e.g., *inby* – inside, *upby* – up the street, *ootby* – outside, *donby* – down the street

Broon

Newcastle Brown Ale

While known as 'Broon' in the north-east, or nicknamed 'Dog', as in 'seeing a man about a dog', Newcastle Brown Ale is widely known as 'Newkie Brown' elsewhere in the UK.

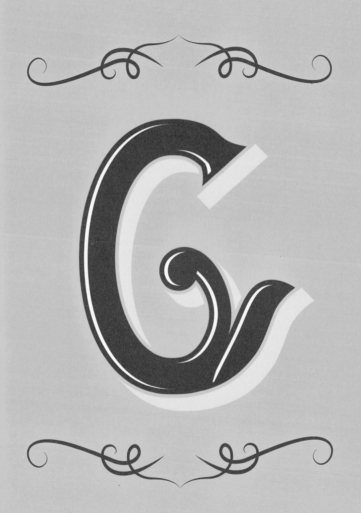

GEORDIE	ENGLISH
cadge	beg, borrow
canna	cannot
canny	good, gentle, kind, likeable and the ultimate Geordie compliment, e.g., *thaas a canny lass*. Also used to mean 'careful' and 'steady'
caps	finishes, e.g., *that caps that*. Originally meant it could not be improved upon
cas	because
champion	used to express delight or wellbeing, as in, 'Eeh, I'm champion, man!'
charva	'chav'
childer	children
claarty	muddy
class	good
claver	gossip

GEORDIE	ENGLISH
cockle	spit
cod	trick, deceive
cowee-handed	awkward
crabby	bad-tempered
crack	gossip
crackin	excellent
cuddy	stupid

clammin'

hungry

'I'm gannin' hyem. I'm clammin' for me bait!'

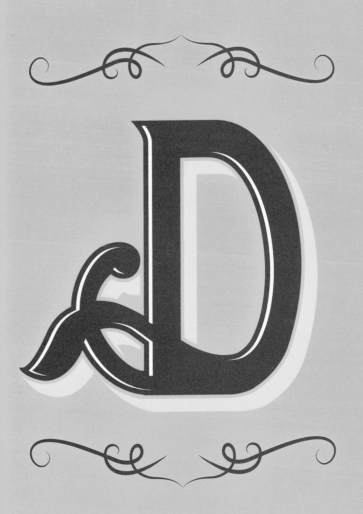

GEORDIE	ENGLISH
daft	silly (sometimes 'daft-like')
deed	dead
deek	look
dinna	do not, e.g., *dinna do that*
div	do (when in front of a vowel or a mute 'h', e.g., *div aah not?*)
divvent	don't
dott'n aboot	lounging
doylem	idiot
draas	trousers (literally 'drawers')
dump	cigarette-end

duds

working-clothes

The use of 'duds' for working-clothes in the north-east predates the American use of the same term.

E·F

ee

eye

'Ee' is an eye in Geordie, but also an exclamation
of surprise, as in 'Ee, dinna do that!'

GEORDIE	ENGLISH
een	eyes
else	already

GEORDIE	ENGLISH
faather	father
faddy	over-particular, especially with food
fashion	(i) resemble, e.g., *he fashions his father*
	(ii) make, e.g., *aal fashion a good un*
fettle	(i) repair, e.g., *aal fettle it*
	(ii) health, mood, e.g., *aam in fine fettle*
	(iii) stop, sort out, e.g., *aal fettle him*
fly	crafty
fower	four
fretish	cold

GEORDIE	ENGLISH
ga	gave (when in front of a consonant, e.g., *ye ga tiv him!*)
gadgie	an old man
gaffer	boss, foreman, supervisor
galloway	horse
gan	gone
gan arn	go ahead
gannin	going, moving, e.g., *gannin along the Scotswood Road*
gannin yem	going home
gassin	talk persistently, gossip
gate	speed
gav	gave (when in front of a vowel, e.g., *he gav it us*)
geen	given, e.g., *aah would geen owt ta seen it*

galloway

horse

Originally a small horse from Galloway in
Scotland, the breed was used to carry lead ore
from the mines to the smelt mills. In Durham, pit
ponies were called galloways, a term subsequently
used for small horses and ponies generally.

GEORDIE	ENGLISH
geet	really
geet walla	very, very large
gi	give (when in front of a consonant)
gis	give me (when in front of a vowel)
giv	See **gis**
giyen	given, e.g., *he's giyen ower much*
gob	mouth
gobby	talkative
gowk	(i) foolish
	(ii) apple core
greet	very
guess	understand (predates the American phrase)

Geordie

inhabitant or dialect of Tyneside

One possible derivation of the word 'Geordie' is the miner's lamp invented by George Stephenson in 1815, which was preferred by local miners. The lamp and then the miners themselves became known as Geordies.

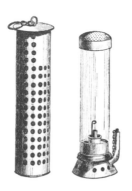

GEORDIE	ENGLISH
haad	grasp, hold, e.g., *take haad on it*
Haddaway, man!	You must be joking!
hanker	hesitate
hereaway	nearby
hevin a gan	having a go
hevyee	have you?
him	he (but used as nominative singular, e.g., *him an me's gannin*)
hinny	canny, when referring to women, girls and children
his	he's

Haddaway!

Go away!

Essentially, 'You must be joking!'
or 'I don't believe you!'

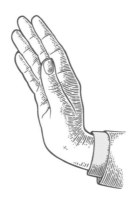

GEORDIE	ENGLISH
hod	hold, e.g., *take hod on it*
hoo	how, e.g., *hoo ye bin the day?*
Howay!	come on (originally shouted when the pit cage was being lowered below ground; nowadays a shout of support for Newcastle United Football Club)
Howay, man!	depending on tone, this could mean 'Hurry up' or 'Get off it'
howfing	large, when used in 'howfing geet'
howk	pick, or scratch
hoy	throw – 'going out on the hoy' means 'going out drinking'
hyem	home

hoose

house

Derived from Old English, typically the ordinary place of residence of a family. The plural is 'hooses'.

GEORDIE	ENGLISH
ingannin	go in
ist	(i) is it?, e.g., *ist fower o'clock?*
	(ii) it is, e.g., *aye ist*
iv	in (when in front of a vowel)
jaa	talk
jannock	fair, honest, genuine
jort	jerk
jye	crooked

Jarra

Jarrow

On 5 October 1936, 200 unemployed men began the Jarrow Crusade to present a petition signed by 12,000 residents of Jarrow to Parliament. Led by David Riley, the chair of the Jarrow council, and Ellen Wilkinson, they walked 282 miles in 26 days.

K·L

GEORDIE	ENGLISH
keek	peep, pry
kelter	condition
ken	(i) know (knowledge)
	(ii) be acquainted with
	(iii) remember
knackered	tired

GEORDIE	ENGLISH
lad	(i) sweetheart (masculine)
	(ii) brother
laddie	boy
lads	friends (not necessarily young men)
lang	long, tall
lass	(i) sweetheart (feminine)
	(ii) wife
lassie	girl
lay	stop, e.g., *lay yer braggin*
leetnin	dawn
load	large quantity

GEORDIE	ENGLISH
maisey	confused
man	(i) husband, e.g., *her man*
	(ii) must, e.g., *aah man away noo*
	(iii) just added to the end of a sentence, e.g., *yor aal reet man*
mangst	among
manny	young man
me	(i) I (used instead of 'I' when it forms the compound subject of a sentence, e.g., *me and her's faalen oot*)
	(ii) when 'me' is emphasised it is pronounced 'meah', e.g., *it wasna meah*

marra

mate or friend, especially workmate
(sometimes shortened to 'mar')

Derived from Old Norse, it's thought that the word was originally used by coal miners in the nineteenth century to mean 'pit pony', then to refer to each other before spreading beyond the mines.

GEORDIE	ENGLISH
mind	(i) be sure
	(ii) beware
	(iii) remember
	(iv) intention, e.g., *aav a mind ter*
	(v) just added to the end of a sentence, e.g., *he's a good lad mind*
minded	intention, e.g., *aam minded ter*
morn	tomorrow
mun	must

mortal

drunk

In use as far back as 1898, 'mortal drunk'
or simply 'mortal' means 'very drunk'. An
alternative is 'mortalious'.

GEORDIE	ENGLISH
na	no (also added to the end of other words to imply negatives, e.g., *henna* – have not, *winna* – will not, *canna* – cannot)
nappa	head
nar	near
nebby	nosey
nee	no, also 'haven't any'
neet	night
netty	toilet
nippy	cold
noo	now
nor	than
nowt	nothing
Nucassel	Newcastle

netty

toilet

Some think that 'netty' may derive from *gabinetto*, the Italian word for toilet, but perhaps more likely is that it is a corruption of 'necessary' as in 'necessary house', meaning privy or toilet.

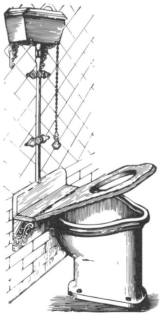

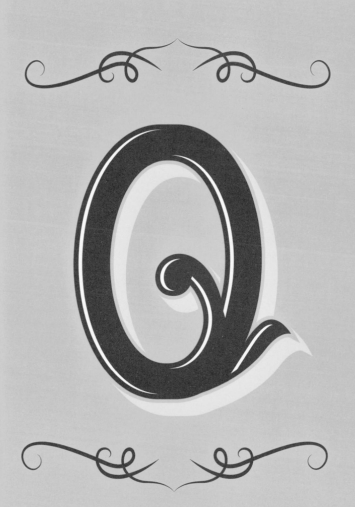

GEORDIE	ENGLISH
off	(i) by
	(ii) from, e.g., *borrad a tenner off him*
on	(i) of, e.g., *what are ye feared on?*
	(ii) busy, e.g., *he's on threshin'*
on't	on it e.g., *look at the legs on't*
or	than, e.g., *rather you or me*
owa	over
ower	too, e.g., *he's ower small fer't pit*
owt	anything
owt mair?	anything else?

outed

become common knowledge

While today 'outed' tends to mean revealing someone's sexual or gender identity against their will, in the past Geordies would use 'outed' of anything which had become public knowledge.

GEORDIE	ENGLISH
paggered	very tired
peel off	get rid of
pelt	hurry along
pet	term of endearment used by both sexes to the other
peth	a road running up a hill
Pitmatic	a form of Geordie spoken in the mines of the north-east
play	out of work, sick from work, e.g., *aas been playin' me fer a week*
ploat	to pluck feathers
plodge	to wade into water
propa	significant
putters	young boys who pushed wheeled coal tubs underground

pollis

police

Simply a regional pronunciation of 'police' but
also a reminder, like the Scottish *polis*, that
the word 'police' is derived from *polis*, a Greek
city-state, particularly its ideal form. Police
represent the *polis*, the state.

Q · R

GEORDIE	ENGLISH
quick	alert
radge	mad
radgie	a particularly aggressive person, a 'chav'. Also a temper tantrum – 'He's gannin' proper radgie' means 'He had a real temper tantrum'
randy	quarrelsome
reet	right
round the doors	nearby

radgie

a temper tantrum

As in, 'He's gannin' proper radgie.'

GEORDIE	ENGLISH
sackless	stupid, hopeless
safe	sure, certain
sand-dancer	an inhabitant of South Shields
sarra	serve, e.g., *did yer sarra yer time i' the yards?*
scabby	shabby
scarry	easily frightened
scrunch	squeeze
scunner	aversion or dislike
seed	saw
seet	sight
sel	self, e.g., *his aan sel.* Often added to other words, e.g., *missel* – myself, *thosel* – yourself, *hissel* – hisself
set	cause, e.g., *yaal set the roof down*, which was a cautionary remark in the pit

sarra

serve

'Did yer sarra yer time i' the yards?' is a reference to the famous shipyards of the north-east. The most famous ship launched from the Swan Hunter yard on the Tyne was RMS *Mauretania*, a transatlantic liner which was launched on 20 September 1906. It was the largest ship in the world until the launch of RMS *Olympic* in 1910.

GEORDIE	ENGLISH
sharp	(i) early
	(ii) cold weather
Sheels	North Shields
shift	(i) shirt
	(ii) move
	(iii) working hours
shuggy-boat	fairground ride, resembling a large swing
shy	(i) unwilling
	(ii) short change
side	put in order
sitha!	look!
skemmy	a low-grade homing pigeon
skemp	short change

skran

food

Provisions or a portion of food carried by a labourer into the field for a meal. In nautical slang, 'cold scran' is cold refreshment.

GEORDIE	ENGLISH
slack	not enough, e.g., *trade's slack*
smerking	smoking
snadgee	swede (vegetable)
step	walk
stewmer	tearaway

snout

cigarette

Some suggest that the word is derived from a
prisoner, when tobacco was banned in prisons,
attempting to hide his smoking by pretending to
rub his nose, others that the word is derived from
the use of snuff, inhaled via the nose, or 'snout'.

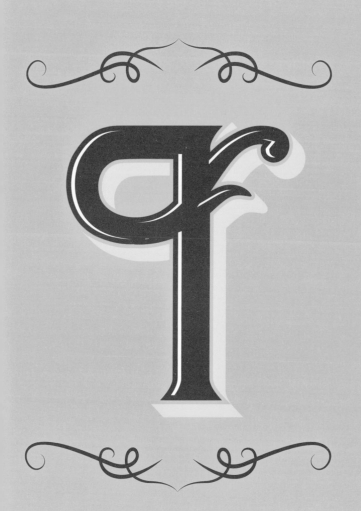

GEORDIE	ENGLISH
tab	cigarette
tackle	take on, e.g., *aal tackle that job*
tally	count
teem	pour
teemin'	raining heavily
ter	to
thaas	you have
that	so, e.g., *it were that dark!*
the	frequently added to other words, e.g., *the noo* – now, *the day* – today, *the neet* – tonight, *the morn* – tomorrow

tatie

potato

Geordie Tatie Pot was a traditional Second World War and post-war recipe, cooking leftover Sunday roast in the oven with potatoes, a carrot, an onion and leftover gravy.

GEORDIE	ENGLISH
think on	remember
thor	(i) their
	(ii) they are
thumpin'	large
ti	to (when in front of a consonant, e.g., *aal gannin ti toon*)
tiv	to (when in front of a vowel, e.g., *aal gannin tiv aar hoose*)
towsher	scruffy

toon

town, Newcastle

Newcastle is known as 'the Toon', due to the
Geordie pronunciation of 'town'. Its football
team's supporters are known as the Toon Army.

U·V

GEORDIE	ENGLISH
us	(i) me
	(ii) we
varnigh	very nearly
varra	very
vennel	the word for a narrow alley in Durham

up a heyt

up in the air

While 'up a heyt' can mean literally 'high up',
it can also mean 'upset' or 'angry'.

W·Y

W·Y

GEORDIE	ENGLISH
wadden	would not
walla	very large
wants	need, e.g., *aah wants a job*
war!	look out!
wazzock	idiot
whey	(i) then, e.g., *wi gannin whey?*
	(ii) well, e.g., *whey aam gannin*
whey aye	definitely, e.g., *whey eye aam gannin*
whyeye	yes
wi	(i) us
	(ii) with (when in front of a consonant, e.g., *gannin wi me*)
	(iii) will

whisht!

be quiet!

A sound often used in some form to calm livestock,
in Scotland and Ireland as well as in the north-east
of England, this means 'Hush!' or 'Be quiet!'

GEORDIE	ENGLISH
winnet	will not
wor	our
worsels	ourselves
wrang	wrong
ya	you
yammer	talk incessantly
ye bugger mar	an all-purpose expression that covers surprise, astonishment and pleasure
yee	you
yem	home – see also **hyem**
yer	you
yous	you (plural)

Wey aye, man!

Yes!

Enthusiastic agreement.
Also 'Wey aye, pet!' As in, 'Ye gannin yem?'
'Wey aye, man!'

ENGLISH

-

GEORDIE

ENGLISH	GEORDIE
afraid	afeard
aggressive person	radgie
alert	quick
all	aal
alley (narrow, in Durham)	vennel
along	alang
already	else
also	an aal
among	mangst
animal, small	beastie
anything	owt
anything else?	owt mair?
apple core	gowk
autumn	backeend
aversion	scunner
awkward	aakwad
awkward (shy)	blate
awkward (unco-ordinated)	cowee-handed

ENGLISH	GEORDIE
bad (used ironically)	bonny
bad-tempered	crabby
be quiet!	whisht!
beaten	bested
because	cas
become common knowledge	outed
beg	cadge
been	bin
behind	aback
between	atween
beware	mind
borrow	cadge
boss	gaffer
boy	laddie
brother	lad
busy	on
by	off
by (in front of a consonant)	bi
by (in front of a vowel)	biv
by this time	binno

ENGLISH	GEORDIE
cannot	canna
canny	hinny (of women, girls and children)
cause	set
certain	safe
'chav'	charva
children	childer
cigarette	snout, tab
cigarette-end	dump
cold	fretish, nippy
cold weather	early
Come off it!	Howay, man!
Come on!	Howay!
condition	kelter
confused	maisey
count	tally
crafty	fly
crooked	jye

ENGLISH	GEORDIE
dawn	leetnin
dead	deed
deceive	cod
definitely	whey aye
delighted	champion
dinner	bait
dislike	scunner
do	div
do not	dinna, divvent
drunk	mortal

ENGLISH	GEORDIE
early	sharp
endure	bide
excellent (adj.)	crackin'
excellent (of a person or thing)	bobby dazzler
eye(s)	ee, een (plural)

ENGLISH	GEORDIE
fair	jannock
fairground ride, resembling a large swing	shuggy-boat
father	faather
fellow	beggar
finishes	caps
food	skran
foolish	gowk
football	baal
for	at
foreman	gaffer
four	fower
frail	brockle
friend	marra
friends	lads
frightened, easily	scarry
from	off

ENGLISH	GEORDIE
gave (in front of a consonant)	ga
gave (in front of a vowel)	gav
gentle	canny
genuine	jannock
get rid of	peel off
getting worse	back-gannin
give (in front of a consonant)	gi
give me (in front of a vowel)	gis, giv
given	geen, giyen
glad	blythe
go ahead	gan arn
Go away!	Haddaway!
go in	ingannin
going	gannin
going home	gannin yem
gone	gan
good	canny, class
good, really	belta
good-looking	bonny
gossip	claver, crack, gassin
grasp	haad

ENGLISH	GEORDIE
have you?	hevyee
having a go	hevin a gan
he	him
head	nappa
health	fettle
he's	his
hesitate	hanker
himself	hissel
hold	haad, hod
home	hyem, yem
homing pigeon (low-grade)	skemmy
honest	jannock
hopeless	sackless
horse	galloway
house	hoose
how	hoo
hungry	clamming
hurry along	pelt
Hurry up!	Howay, man!
husband	man

ENGLISH	GEORDIE
I	aah, me
I don't believe you!	Haddaway!
I will	aal
idiot	doylem, wazzock
in	at
in (in front of a vowel)	iv
infant	babby
is it?	ist
it is	ist

ENGLISH	GEORDIE
Jarrow	Jarra
jerk	jort

ENGLISH	GEORDIE
kind	canny
know	ken

ENGLISH	GEORDIE
large	howfing, thumpin'
large, very	walla
large, very, very	geet walla
large quantity	load
lassie	girl
likeable	canny
long	lang
look	deek
look!	sitha!
look out!	war!
lounging	dott'n aboot

ENGLISH	GEORDIE
mad	radge
make	fashion
mate	marra
majority	berrer-end
me	us
mine boys	putters
miner's Geordie	Pitmatic
mouth	gob
move	shift
moving	gannin
muddy	claarty
must	man, or mun
myself	missel

ENGLISH	GEORDIE
near	nar
nearby	hereaway, round the doors

ENGLISH	GEORDIE
nearly, very	varnigh
near to	by
need	wants
Newcastle	Nucassel
Newcastle Brown Ale	Broon
next to	aside of, by
night	neet
no	na, nee
North Shields	Sheels
nosey	nebby
not enough	slack
nothing	nowt
now	noo

ENGLISH	GEORDIE
old man	gadgie
old-fashioned	aadfashint
on it	on't
our	wor
ourselves	worsels
out of work	play

ENGLISH	GEORDIE
over	owa
over-particular	faddy
own	aan

ENGLISH	GEORDIE
packed lunch	bait
peep	keek
perfect	bramma
pick	howk
pleasant disposition	bonny
pluck feathers	ploat
police	pollis
poor	badly off
potato	tatie
pour	teem
precarious	brockle
pry	keek
public house	booza
put an end to	cap
put in order	side

ENGLISH	GEORDIE
quarrelsome	randy

ENGLISH	GEORDIE
raining heavily	teemin'
really	geet
remember	ken, mind, think on
repair	fettle
resemble	fashion
return	back-ower
right	reet
road running up a hill	peth

ENGLISH	GEORDIE
saw	seed
scratch	howk
scruffy	towsher
self	sel
serve	sarra
several	amany
shabby	scabby
shirt	shift
short	bit
short change	shy, skemp
shy	blate
sick	bad
sick from work	play
sight	seet
significant	propa
silly	daft
small	bit
smoking	smerking
snack	bait
so	that
sort out	fettle
South Shields inhabitant	sand-dancer
speed	gate
spit	cockle
squeeze	scrunch

ENGLISH	GEORDIE
stop	fettle, lay
stream	beck
stupid	cuddy
supervisor	gaffer
sure	mind, safe
swede (vegetable)	snadgee
sweetheart (male)	lad
sweetheart (female)	lass

ENGLISH	GEORDIE
take on	tackle
talk	jaa
talk incessantly	yammer
talkative	gobby
tall	lang
tearaway	stewmer
term of endearment (m. and f.)	pet
than	nor, or
that	at
their	thor

ENGLISH	GEORDIE
then	whey
they are	thor
throw	hoy
tired	battered, knackered, paggered
to	ter
to (in front of a consonant)	ti
to (in front of a vowel)	tiv
toilet	netty
tomorrow	morn
too	ower
town	toon
trick	cod
trousers	draas
Tyneside dialect	Geordie
Tyneside inhabitant	Geordie

ENGLISH	GEORDIE
uncertain	brockle
underneath	aneath
understand	guess

ENGLISH	GEORDIE
unwilling	shy
up in the air	up a heyt
us	wi

ENGLISH	GEORDIE
very	greet, varra

ENGLISH	GEORDIE
wade into water	plodge
walk	step
well	champion, whey
wife	lass
will	wi

ENGLISH	GEORDIE
will not	winnet
with	wi
working-clothes	duds
working hours	shift
workmate	marra
would not	wadden
wrong	wrang

ENGLISH	GEORDIE
yes	aye, whyeye
yes, but	abbut
yes, of course!	wey aye, man!
you	ya, yee, yer
you (plural)	yous
You don't say!	Haddaway!
you have	thaas
You must be joking!	Haddaway, man!
young child	bairn
young man	manny
yourself	thosel

PRONUNCIATION, GRAMMAR & PUBLIC SPEAKING

PRONUNCIATION

The basic features of spoken Geordie are the cadence of its speech, the quirky tone and the questioning lilt at the end of each sentence.

ENGLISH	GEORDIE

Outstanding in the dialect's pronunciation is the letter 'r', or 'burr' sounded from the tonsils in whatever part of the word the letter occurs. The letter 'a' is a big help. If 'r' is an initial letter, 'a' is added to the start of the word, e.g.:

rain	arrain

roar	arroar

If 'r' is a middle letter, then 'a' is stressed in front of it, e.g.:

early	arly

terrier	tarrier

These are not the only instances of the intrusivenes of 'a', e.g.:

along	alang

amongst	amangst

ENGLISH	GEORDIE

Sometimes at the start of a word:

all	aal
old	aad

Sometimes at the end of a word:

blow	blaa
draw	draa

Other letters can also intrude. One is the letter 'y', which replaces vowels, diphthongs or doubles, e.g.:

pale	pyel
give	gyev
home	hyem
again	agyen
chain	chyen
school	skyul
boot	byut
cook	cyuk

ENGLISH	GEORDIE

Sometimes 'o' alone can intrude:

dare	dore
her	hor
bird	bord
earth	orth

While 'oo' has no difficulty, e.g.:

out	oot
about	aboot
down	doon
strange	stroonge

Neither has 'ee', e.g.:

great	greet
head	heed
sight	seet
do	dee

ENGLISH	GEORDIE

The letter 'w' often appears suddenly in the middle of a word, e.g.:

roll	rowl

hold	howld

Diphthongs are popular (e.g., 'master' becomes **maister**), yet they can easily be ignored.

The letter 'b' is sometimes dropped before 'e' or 'le', although occasionally 'b' is substituted for a 'v', e.g.:

humble	hummel

timber	timmer

rivet	ribet

Be careful when letters suddenly change places – both ways, e.g.:

'd' to 'th' ('fodder' to **'fother'**)

'th' to 'd' ('smithy' to **'smiddy'**)

GRAMMAR

The structure of Geordie sentences contains some features that are common to other dialects, but many are unique to Geordie.

Geordie is a fully-fledged dialect, definitely not a lazy language. The word 'the' is seldom shortened to 't'. It is spoken lightly, in full, and is often placed unexpectedly in front of other words.

Geordie contains certain verbs that are absent from standard English, e.g., **'gan'**, **'div'** and **'wi'**. Some words are never used in Geordie – 'may' becomes **'can'** or **'might'**, while 'shall' becomes **'will'** (except in the first person question, e.g., *shall I have a look?*).

Certain Geordie words are a constant reminder of past English, e.g.:

'those' becomes **'them'**

'which' becomes **'what'**

'because' becomes **'being as'**

'in order to' becomes **'for to'**

Negatives are where regional dialects are most expressive and Geordie is no exception, with a definite grammar of its own, e.g.:

(i) 'impossible' means 'can't', but is changed to 'mustn't' (pronounced '**musna**')

(ii) 'forbidden' means 'mustn't', but is changed to 'haven't got to' (pronounced '**hevna got ta**')

(iii) 'unnecessary' means 'haven't got to', but is changed to 'don't have to' (pronounced '**dinna hev ta**')

Normally, the word 'never' is used to mean 'not under any circumstances', but the Geordie dialect uses it to say things like 'I never went to the match'. And, of course, there is the omnipresent double negative such as 'I wouldn't have none of it.'

Questions are another area where Geordie has its own sentence construction, e.g.:

(i) 'You're not ready are you?' becomes '**You're not ready aren't you?**'

(ii) 'You're ready aren't you?' becomes '**You're ready are you?**'

Finally, there are other grammatical constructions illustrative of Geordie, e.g.:

(i) the personal pronoun is repeated at the end of the sentence, e.g., *ya young monkey ya*

(ii) the subject is placed at the end of the sentence, e.g., *they've won agyen the lads*

(iii) The third person is misplaced, e.g., *me and me marra*

PUBLIC SPEAKING

Now you are ready for a few Geordie phrases. Here are some important ones to listen out for:

GEORDIE	ENGLISH
How abott byen a Broon?	It's your round.
Een doon lukkin.	The bingo is about to start.
Shut yor gob.	Please keep quiet.
Yegot neh yem te ganti?	Please leave.
Heya hard mi?	Didn't you catch my previous remark?
in a fettle boiler-shop	in a foul mood

Why not try these out on some Geordie friends?

ENGLISH	GEORDIE
Giz a deek?	Can I have a look?
What ye uptee the neet?	What are you doing **tonight**?
What fettle the day?	How are you?
Nowt but canny.	Very well, thank you.
Lets howay doon tha booza.	Allow me to take you for a drink.
Broons aal roond.	Drinks on me.
Mind yor kiddin!	I don't believe you.

PICTURE CREDITS